CHARLIE RUSSELL
JOURNAL

CHARLIE RUSSELL
JOURNAL

WITH ILLUSTRATIONS BY CHARLES M. RUSSELL

THE COWBOY ARTIST

Montana Historical Society Press
Helena

Cover image: Details, *Charles M. Russell and His Friends*, by Charles M. Russell (1922, oil on canvas, 42" × 81"), Mackay Collection, Montana Historical Society, Helena

Half title page: "Cowboy Mounted #2," 1911, Montana Historical Society, Gift of Barbara J. Schmidt in memory of Kenneth F. and Alice E. MacDonald

Title page: Untitled, c. 1895 (ink with white lead), Montana Historical Society, Gift of Mark H. Brown

Sources for excerpts:
C. M. Russell Museum, Great Falls, Montana: Letters to Fairbanks, May 1921; and Trigg, March 27, 1924. Gilcrease Museum, Tulsa, Oklahoma: Letter to Cole, September 26, 1926. Gund Collection of Western Art, Princeton, New Jersey: Letter to Abbott, May 13, 1919. *Jordan Gazette*, Montana Newspaper Association Inserts: "An Appreciation of Edgar S. Paxson," November 24, 1919. Montana Historical Society, Helena, Montana: Letters to Rance, April 24, 1901; Farr, March 12, 1919; Bogy, July 1, 1925; Lapeyre, August 15, 1925; McDowell, March 28, 1925 and March 14, 1926; and Christmas card, 1926. Stark Museum of Art, Orange, Texas: Letters to Kendall, November 26, 1919; Speck, May 18, 1923; and Goodwin, April 30, 1924. Taylor Museum, Colorado Springs Fine Arts Center, Colorado: "A Few Words About Myself," 1925. The remainder of the letters are in private collections or the location of the original is unknown. Published anthologies of Russell's letters include *Good Medicine* (Garden City, New York, 1930) and *Charles M. Russell, Word Painter*, edited by Brian W. Dippie (Fort Worth, Texas, 1993).

Images from Russell's Western Types Series—*The Trapper, The Post Trader, The Scout #4, The Road Agent, A French Half-Breed, The Stage Driver*, and *Squaw With Bullboat*—are reproduced courtesy of the *Great Falls Tribune*.

Cover design by Arrow Graphics
Book design by Kathryn Fehlig
Printed by Thomson-Shore, Inc., Dexter, Michigan

Distributed by Globe Pequot Press, 246 Goose Lane, Guilford, Connecticut 06437 (800) 243-0495

© 1997 Montana Historical Society Press
P.O. Box 201201, Helena, Montana 59620-1201

08 09 10 11 12 13 14 15   9 8 7 6 5 4 3 2

ISBN-10 0-9759196-6-0
ISBN-13 978-0-9759196-6-8

Preface

Charles Marion Russell (1864–1926) came to Montana at the age of sixteen hoping to become a cowboy. His prominent St. Louis family reluctantly agreed to the trip believing that it would end Charlie's lifelong fascination with the West. It did not. Although "Kid Russell" eventually gave up cowboying to devote his full attention to art, Montana remained home to the celebrated cowboy artist for the rest of his life.

Russell arrived in Montana in time to witness the passing of the Old West and the transformation of the frontier into a place of myth and legend. He knew firsthand the cowboys who had trailed longhorns from Texas and became folk heroes in the process. He was a welcomed guest in the camps of Native Americans who had followed the buffalo before the establishment of reservations altered their way of life forever.

With brush and palette Russell transformed his early experiences in Montana into a splendid vision of the West that once was. Although the exact number is unknown, it is estimated that Russell produced over four thousand works of art during his lifetime. Understandably, he is best known for the masterpieces of frontier life vividly rendered in oils and watercolors. Just as compelling, however, are Russell's works in other media, like his pen and ink drawings. Although lesser-known, these images also capture the spirit and adventure of the West that Russell loved.

It was not just art, however, that brought Russell fame. As intriguing to most was Russell the man—his colorful personality, integrity, and quick wit. Although Russell claimed to be "lame with a pen" when it came to the written word, nothing better illustrates his magnetic character, and his feelings for Montana, than his writings—the stories that he published in books and newspapers and the letters that he wrote to friends.

This journal provides you with glimpses of Russell's artistry with the pen, both as an illustrator and as a "word painter." The drawings are reproduced from the collections of the Montana Historical Society and its fellow institutions devoted to preserving Russell's legacy. A number of the sketches originated as book illustrations. All tell a story. Like the accompanying text, many of them exemplify the unique brand of good humor with which Russell viewed the world. Few people have seen the four untitled drawings included here, which, in all likelihood, have not been published before.

The quotations are excerpted from a variety of sources. Most come from illustrated letters painstakingly written by Russell and highly prized by lucky recipients. Several were taken from "A Few Words About Myself," a short autobiographical essay written by the artist toward the end of his life and used to preface the published collections of his stories, *More Rawhides* and *Trails Plowed Under*. Punctuation and capitalization were added where necessary to make the excerpts comprehensible. In all other cases Russell's original style was copied exactly to retain the distinct flavor created by the artist's blatant disregard for the conventions of spelling and grammar.

Russell's writings and sketches are presented together in this journal to inspire you. May they encourage you—like Russell—to record your visions of the world around you in words and pictures.

Kirby Lambert
Curator of Collections, Montana Historical Society, Helena

Pete Had a Winning Way with Cattle, 1921
Montana Historical Society, Gift of C. R. Smith

Cow folks are scarce now ... but thiy left tracks in history
that the farmer cant plow under.

Letter to George W. Farr, March 12, 1919

The Trapper, 1901
Montana Historical Society, Mackay Collection

He loved the Old West, and those who love her I count as friends.

"An Appreciation of Edgar S. Paxson"

Waiting, c. 1911
C. M. Russell Museum, Great Falls, Montana

The West is dead! You may lose a sweetheart,
but you won't forget her.

Foreword to *Good Medicine*

The Geyser Busts Loose, 1917
Montana Historical Society, Gift of C.R. Smith

Woldent you like to get a horse under you and ride over som real grass country and get down on your belly and drink from a cold mountion stream?

Letter to Dick Bodkin, May 20, 1925

The Initiation of the Tenderfoot, c. 1899
Rockwell Museum, Corning, New York

Life has never been verry serious
with me—I lived to play and I'm playing yet.

"A Few Words About Myself," 1925

The Post Trader, 1901
Montana Historical Society, Mackay Collection

If you want the big hills that ware white robes and where the teeth of the world tear holes in the clouds the trail to my lodge is not grass grone and my pipe will be lit for you.

Letter to Philip R. Goodwin, April 30, 1924

The Odds Looked About Even, 1925
Montana Historical Society, Mackay Collection

Heres hoping the worst end of your trail is behind you ...

Russell's 1926 Christmas card

The Scout #4, 1901
Montana Historical Society, Mackay Collection

To me the roar of a mountian stream mingled with the bells of a pack trane is grander musick than all the string or brass bands in the world.

Letter to Mike Shannon, June 17, 1923

From the Southwest Comes Spanish an' Mexican Traders, 1926
Montana Historical Society, Mackay Collection

The old time cow man right now is as much history as Richard,
The Lion Harted or any of those gents that packed a long blade
and had their cloths made by a blacksmith.

Letter to Douglas Fairbanks, Jr. , May 1921

Indians in Pirogue, c. 1911
Amon Carter Museum, Fort Worth, Texas

The Red man was the true American. They have almost gon.
but will never be forgotten.

Inscription for Joe De Yong, 1916

The Land He Owned
Buffalo Bill Historical Center, Cody, Wyoming

Civilization is nature's worst enemy.
All wild things vanish when she comes.

"An Appreciation of Edgar S. Paxson"

Untitled, c. 1899
Montana Historical Society, Museum Purchase, Great Falls Elks Club Collection

Old Ma Nature was kind to her red children
and the old time cow puncher was her adopted son.

Letter to E. C. "Teddy Blue" Abbott, May 13, 1919

Most of the Cow Ranches I've Seen Lately Was Like a Big Farm, 1925
Montana Historical Society, Gift of C. R. Smith

Laughs and good judgment have saved me maney a black eye.

"A Few Words About Myself," 1925

Old-Man Saw a Crane Flying Over The Land, 1920
Montana Historical Society, Gift of C. R. Smith

And when it coms to making the beautiful Ma nature
has man beat all ways from the ace
and that old lady still owns a lot of montana.

Letter to Philip G. Cole, September 26, 1926

Lady Bronc Rider, c. 1925
C. M. Russell Museum, Great Falls, Montana

Evolutionist say it took Millions of years to turn a monky to a man and Every body knows that a women can make a monkey out of a man in a fiew hours . . . Evolution is dam slow.

Letter to Edwin G. Lapeyre, August 15, 1925

When Nature's Store Seemed Endless, n.d.
Buffalo Bill Historical Center, Cody, Wyoming

Like most men of my age my harte lives back on trails
that have been plowed under.

Letter to Sam E. McDowell, March 14, 1926

The Virginian, c. 1911
Amon Carter Museum, Fort Worth, Texas

Betwine the pen and the brush there is little diffornce
but I belive the man that makes word pictures is the greater.

Letter to Ralph S. Kendall, November 26, 1919

In the Old Days the Cow Ranch Wasn't Much, 1925
Montana Historical Society, Mackay Collection

Lonesumniss makes strong friends of shy strangers.

Letter to Edward Borein, 1916

The Road Agent, 1901
Montana Historical Society, Mackay Collection

Xmas has past. Santy Claus has come an gon leaving us all broke but happy. If he wasent so plesent about it Id call him a holdup.

Letter to John N. Marchand, December 29, 1905

The Mountains and Plains Seemed to Stimulate a Man's Imagination, 1926
Montana Historical Society, Mackay Collection

In the city men shake hands and call each other friends
but its the lonsome places that ties their harts together
and harts do not forget.

Letter to Tom Conway, March 24, 1917

A French Half-Breed, 1901
Montana Historical Society, Museum Purchase

I have a camp in the Glacier park where the pipe is [lit] and the robe spred for you aneytime you come.

Letter to Will James, May 30, 1924

Mosquito Season in Cascade, 1896
Montana Historical Society, Gift of Mrs. Charles Sheridan in memory of Mrs. Ben Roberts

Old Dad Time trades little that men want. He has traded me wrinkles for teeth stiff legs for limber ones . . . [but] he has left me my friends and for that great Kindness I forgive him.

Letter to Josephine Trigg, March 27, 1924

Rawhide Rawlins, Mounted, 1925
Montana Historical Society, Mackay Collection

Any man that likes a Cyuse is a friend of mine
. . . I never knew a horse lover that was a mean man.

Letter to Sam E. McDowell, March 28, 1925

Looks at the Stars, 1920
Montana Historical Society, Gift of C. R. Smith

Aney man that can mak a living doing
what he likes is lucky an I'm that.

"A Few Words About Myself," 1925

About the Third Jump Con Loosens, 1921
Montana Historical Society, Mackay Collection

I had friends when I had nothing else.

"A Few Words About Myself," 1925

Untitled, c. 1899
Montana Historical Society, Museum Purchase, Great Falls Elks Club Collection

I hope when you look
    at This sketch it will not your modesty shock
For we've both Been There many a Time
when we roomed in The Canary Block. —

The best towns in Montana started with whiskey and hitching racks. Its a sinch it wasent Co Co Cola and Garages.

Letter to Louis V. Bogy, July 1, 1925

The Stage Driver, 1901
Montana Historical Society, Museum Purchase

I was at the beach the other day—and if truth gose naked like
they say it dos folks dont lye much at the sea shore.

Letter to George Speck, May 18, 1923

Like a Flash They Turned, 1925
Montana Historical Society, Mackay Collection

For a steady thing give me Montana.

Letter to Bill Rance, April 24, 1901

Squaw with Bullboat, 1901
Montana Historical Society, Museum Purchase

Good medicine to you and yours...

Letter to Harry Stanford, May 8, 1925

Flatboat on River, Fort [Union] in Background, 1925
Montana Historical Society, Gift of C. R. Smith

Good friends make the roughest trail Easy.

Letter to Josephine Trigg, March 27, 1924

Cowboy Seated, Horse Nuzzling His Left Hand, 1911
Montana Historical Society, Mackay Collection

Untitled, c. 1895
Montana Historical Society, Gift of Mark H. Brown